A call for Christian thinking and action
The life of Raymond Johnston

David Holloway

GW00501490

CHRISTIAN INFLUENCE IN A SECULAR WORLD

This paper was originally given as a lecture in The Christian Institute's Autumn Lecture series on November 5th 2001 at St Stephen's Church, Elswick, Newcastle upon Tyne.

Copyright © The Christian Institute 2004

The author has asserted his right under Section 77 of the Copyright, Designs & Patents Act 1988 to be identified as the author of this work.

First printed in January 2004

ISBN 1 901 086 24-0

Published by The Christian Institute
Wilberforce House, 4 Park Road, Gosforth Business Park,
Newcastle upon Tyne, NE12 8DG

The Christian Institute is a Company Limited by Guarantee, registered in England as a charity. Company No. 263 4440, Charity No. 100 4774.
A charity registered in Scotland. Charity No. SC039220

Contents

Introduction

On 25 October 1985 this obituary was recorded in *The Times* newspaper. It was the obituary on Raymond Johnston. It read as follows:

> Mr Raymond Johnston, the director of CARE Trust (formerly the Nationwide Festival of Light), died after a short illness on October 17. He was 58.
>
> Following the formation of the Nationwide Festival of Light, he became its first director in 1974. The NFOL was essentially a Christian grass roots movement of protest against certain changes in sexual and social morality that began in the 1960s. As director, he gave intellectual and political weight to a movement that had quiet but considerable influence. Much of his time was spent in research, writing, briefings, and coordination of campaigns. His submissions and responses to Home Office or DHSS committees inquiring into matters of moral and ethical concern were always models of careful argument and clarity. In the last year of his life he had been campaigning for the protection of the human embryo in the light of the Warnock Report.
>
> As a strong Evangelical Anglican he was convinced that a strong family structure was essential for a healthy society. His 1978 London Lectures in Contemporary Christianity 'Who Needs the Family?' spelt this out and show how all his thinking was deeply rooted in a biblical Christian faith.

Raymond Johnston was born on April 4, 1927. After Solihull School, The Queen's College, Oxford (where he read modern languages), and studying theology at the London Bible College, he taught modern languages in schools in Kent and Sheffield. From 1964 to 1974 he was a lecturer in the Department of Education at the University of Newcastle-upon-Tyne.

While at Newcastle, he began his involvement in the central affairs of the Church of England. A churchwarden of Jesmond parish church, he was elected from the diocese of Newcastle to the Church Assembly (now the General Synod) from 1965 to 1970.

After leaving Newcastle in 1974 to become director of the Nationwide Festival of Light, he was returned to the House of Laity of the General Synod as a member for Oxford from 1980 to 1985 … His speeches in Synod debates were always respected for their honesty and candidness.

He is survived by his wife, Peggy, and their two daughters.

I actually wrote that obituary, having known Raymond personally since 1972. That was when I was interviewed for the post of vicar of Jesmond in Newcastle upon Tyne. At the time he was one of the two churchwardens at Jesmond Parish Church.

I simply want to say, by way of introduction, something briefly about Raymond the man. I will then focus on Raymond's beliefs and concerns.

At the memorial service for Raymond Johnston Dr J I Packer – who was a life-long, or more precisely since-student-days friend – described Raymond Johnston as "one of God's Barnabas's". Dr Packer was referring to Acts 11.23-24 and Barnabas' visit to Antioch where we read:

"… he [Barnabas] was glad and encouraged them all to remain true to the Lord with all their hearts. He was a good man, full of the Holy Spirit and faith."

And Raymond *was* constantly "encouraging" people "to remain true to the Lord with all their hearts". He was "a good man, full of the Holy Spirit and faith."

But Raymond was not stuffy. He had a great sense of humour. In his book *Caring and Campaigning* he wrote:

> A Christian who has no sense of humour should pray for one! And those who rejoice in such a gift should pray that the Lord will help them to use it to good advantage.

Raymond was a man of wide sympathies and interests. He was a lover of the arts. In that respect he was a genuine Christian humanist in the tradition of C.S.Lewis who he greatly respected. He loved music. He was on the board of the Northern Symphonia and was instrumental in getting Christopher Seaman as the conductor after the departure of Rudolph Schwartz. He loved good painting, good architecture and good broadcasting. That inevitably made him oppose all that was bad and demeaning in the arts. Indeed, he not only campaigned against pornography. He also opposed some of the monstrosities – for example, tower blocks – that came to desecrate our cities in the 60s and 70s.

And Raymond was concerned for the whole person. He was not just someone who saw people as "spiritual" and so merely targets for evangelism. No! He was a great "scouter". Yes, he used his scouting as an opportunity for Christian witness and teaching but not in any exploitative way. It is probably due to Raymond Johnston that scouts [and guides and all the other groups] have continued to this day as effective groups at Jesmond Parish Church.

Nor must we forget his loyal support of Newcastle United Football Club. There was Raymond on most Saturdays (if there was a home game), exercising his lungs in support of the "Toon", in the days, of course, of "Super-Mac" – Malcolm Macdonald – rather than of Kevin Keegan or of Alan Shearer. My memories of Raymond's exploits as a fan include an occasion in the early seventies when soccer was beginning to turn "nasty" in terms of "terrace behaviour".

I switched on the early evening TV news to get the final score of, I think, Newcastle at home to Nottingham Forrest. What should I see but headline news relating to that very match for there had been a pitch invasion - something quite unknown in those days. Inevitably there was condemnation of this hooligan behaviour. But who should be filmed in the fore-front of the spectators running along the pitch but Raymond Johnston. It was hilarious, seeing the middle-aged future director of the Nationwide Festival of Light, the champion of discipline in schools, as large as life running with all the yobs! The truth, of course, was, as I found out when I teased him in church the next day, that fighting had broken out in his stand; so people like himself sitting or standing near the front were forced onto the pitch by the physical force of the crowd pressure from behind.

In the same way as he "theologised" (and fairly) his love of humour, he "sociologised" (equally fairly) his loyalty to Newcastle United:

> It is worth remarking [he wrote] how the need for local allegiances, which is denied by the dreary monochrome of so much of our standardized existence in modern bureaucratic industrial society, is today expressed in the colourful world of sport, and particularly of supporters' clubs. To be a football "fan", for example, may in one sense be part of discovering one's local identity… We all need to know where we belong in space and time.

So much for Raymond the man. I now want to turn to his beliefs and concerns. And I want to draw attention to three aspects of these that, I believe, are still vital for today. So I have three headings or propositions. *First*, Raymond Johnston was rooted in the Bible and the 16th Century Reformers; *secondly*, Raymond Johnston focused on cultural disintegration; and, *thirdly*, Raymond Johnston called for Christian thinking and action.

Rooted in the Bible and the 16th Century Reformers

Raymond Johnston came to faith through the ministry of Dick True and the other leaders at the Solihull Crusader Class. It was there that he received his basic Christian nurture. That gave Raymond his understanding of the supreme authority of the Bible. Raymond was, indeed, a biblical Christian. He wanted to know what Jesus and the Apostles taught, not what the latest speculations of some eccentric religious guru might be.

But Raymond did not just accept the authority of the Bible and leave open how it should be interpreted. No! He believed in "the perspicuity of the Scripture". You don't need the Church or independent human reason to unlock the Bible. Yes, they can help. But the basic content of the Bible is clear enough. This was a fundamental tenet of the Reformation and Raymond followed that Reformed understanding. Here is how Martin Luther expresses it:

> I certainly grant that many *passages* in the Scripture are obscure and hard to elucidate, but that is due, not to the exalted nature of their subject, but to our own linguistic and grammatical ignorance; and it does not in any way prevent our knowing all the *contents* of Scripture.

And Luther goes on:

> The perspicuity of Scripture is twofold … The first is external, and relates to the ministry of the Word; the second concerns the knowledge of the heart. If you speak of *internal* perspicuity, the truth is that nobody who has not the Spirit of God sees a jot of what is in the Scriptures. All men have their hearts darkened, so that, even when they can discuss and quote all that is in Scripture, they do not understand or really know any of it … the Spirit is needed for the understanding of all Scripture and every part of Scripture. If on the other hand you speak of *external* perspicuity, the position is that nothing whatsoever is left obscure or ambiguous, but all that is in the Scripture is through the Word brought forth into the clearest light and proclaimed to the whole world.

Now, I have given you that extended quotation because it comes from the first book that Raymond Johnston was responsible for – a translation of Luther's *The Bondage of the Will*, which he jointly translated with Jim Packer and for which together with Jim Packer he wrote the very helpful introduction. This claimed that *The Bondage of the Will* is "the greatest piece of writing that came from Luther's pen." The book makes Raymond's own theology so clear as it makes so clear what was at the heart of the Reformation – namely the sovereignty and grace of God on the one hand and the sinfulness of men and women on the other hand. That sinfulness had so "bound the human will" that human beings were helpless in doing anything to save themselves. Unless God stepped in to empower them, they were without hope. But the gospel is that God has stepped in in Christ on the cross and through the Holy Spirit who opens blind eyes and generates faith. This issue of the "bondage of the will" Luther claimed was "the hinge on which all turns."

But how did this Reformed thinking come out in Raymond's own basic theology? He gives us a good summary of the issues, not long before he died, in his little book *Nationhood: towards a Christian Perspective*:

Every Protestant Confession asserts the sovereign control of God in providence over every event in time, in accordance with the teaching of the Old Testament prophets, of our Lord himself (eg Matthew 10.29 – "Are not two sparrows sold for a penny? Yet not one of them will fall to the ground apart from the will of your Father") and of the New Testament epistles (eg Ephesians 1.11 – "In him we were also chosen, having been predestined according to the plan of him who works out everything in conformity with the purpose of his will"). The Christian is meant to live with confidence in the hand of God, who sustains and governs all things, rather than as a prey to the message of meaninglessness so prevalent today, or to any version of the juggernaut evolutionary theory. God sustains and rules.

Sustaining is more than maintaining – it is rather an active grip which holds everything together (Col 1.17 – "He [Jesus Christ] is before all things, and in him all things hold together"), an energizing upholding (Heb 1.3 – "The Son is the radiance of God's glory and the exact representation of his being, sustaining all things by his powerful word") without which all things would disintegrate into unimagined chaos and darkness … [It is] God's active rule or government. Nations exist by and under his providential sustaining power … but they also emerge, develop and fall according to his sovereign purpose.

Neither in the case of individuals nor in the case of nations does providence rule out responsibility. Men and communities are held accountable for their rebellion against the law written in their own hearts, idolatry, violence and other forms of wickedness. [Yes] evil is woven into the divine plan and can mysteriously be turned to good, as supremely in the death of Jesus, boldly announced by the apostles as bringing both deadly guilt and a glorious salvation (Acts 2.23; 3.15; 4.28).

Raymond Johnston believed that the 16th century Reformers needed to be rediscovered. After all they themselves were only rediscovering apostolic Christianity. And Raymond Johnston not only believed, he acted. Jim Packer tells us how:

Raymond went to the IVF General Conference at Swanick [when he and Raymond were students together at Oxford in the late 40s] and came back raving about the speaker he heard there named Lloyd Jones. Also he discovered for himself the writings of Bishop J C Ryle and through Ryle the seventeenth century Puritan writers. Then he introduced me to them – that's something for which I can never thank him enough. Incidentally it was Raymond who first thought of holding an annual Puritan Studies Conference in London and who in 1949 took me to meet Dr Lloyd Jones whom I didn't know at that time, so that we might enlist his help. That too, seems to me in retrospect, to have been a momentous action on Raymond's part.

Now it was because Raymond was a "Reformation man" that he saw no dichotomy between his Christian faith and social concern. The doctrine of the Sovereignty of God means that God is concerned for the whole of life, not just life on Sundays in church but Monday to Saturday out in the world as well. He believed that God was creator as well as redeemer; and he believed this created world couldn't be neglected even though our attitude towards it must always be in the light of heaven and eternity. He believed that God had created man in his own image, and that although that image was distorted by sin, it hadn't been destroyed. He, therefore, believed in the sanctity of human life. Believing also that "the archetypal transgression was murder" as evidenced in the sin of Cain, he naturally campaigned against attacks on human life. And the great attack since 1967 he saw coming through abortion, that huge blot on the moral landscape.

Let me give you Raymond's reasoning on this subject in some detail as it is still something to be fought and campaigned against. I quote:

> The question that is raised is: is it, or is it not, murder? It is true that the Bible never mentions deliberate induced abortion, so there is no explicit ruling on the matter. Nevertheless, by the end of the first century, one of the Christian ethical distinctives was already that Christians did not practise abortion. The *Didache*, an early manual of moral teaching and guide to conduct, was probably written before some of the latest epistles in the New Testament: it is against abortion. A prohibition against abortion was among the … canons of the Council of Elvira (c AD 306).

By the end of the second century, the influence of Christianity had brought Roman law to forbid abortion, long before the conversion of Constantine and the Christianizing of the Roman Empire. Long before that, under the Emperor Severus, Roman law forbade abortion. This was the influence of Christianity over a hundred and fifty years. And the medical profession has never wavered over the last two thousand years – until our own lifetime … In Britain, for centuries a pregnant woman convicted of a capital offence could not be hanged – because she was bearing another life …

The key question [then] is this: is the unborn child (for me as a Christian and equally as a member of the human race) entitled to my brotherly, neighbourly protection? Is it entitled to the same protection I would seek to give to a person I saw being attacked in the street? Is the unborn child my neighbour – or not?

Raymond Johnston offers five considerations to help us answer that question.

First, *ignorance points only one way*. If our answer is "I do not know", or if I hold that there must be a point between conception and childbirth when the child becomes worthy of my protection but that I do not know when that point is – in either of these cases of ignorance, it must follow that we have to protect the child from the moment of conception onwards, because you could not accept ignorance as a morally valid defence in any comparable case.

Consider the case of a man lying in the street, having been run over or knocked down. You would not say, "I wonder if he is dead or not? I do not know. So I'll leave him, I won't try to save his life, I won't even call the ambulance." On the contrary, you would say that *because* you did not know, you would go straight to that man's aid and help him as much as you could … [similarly] I begin my protection of that child from the moment of conception, simply because I do not know, and because otherwise I could be making a terrible mistake.

Secondly, *human life is genetically complete at conception*.

Admittedly, at the beginning you did not look much like a human being, though we now know that after a few weeks in the womb, you did. In any case, the fact that a person does not look like a human being is not an argument for not protecting him. If you are a doctor called to a major disaster, you do not discuss whether somebody looks enough like a human being before being treated. You just give the treatment …

Thirdly, no criterion of "full humanity" will justify induced abortion. *There is no point at which you can say that you are fully human …*

Fourthly, *human life is a continuum in which birth is only one event.* What is natural birth today could have been induced childbirth yesterday … Indeed, the baby born by natural birth today could have been delivered by caesarean section a month ago…

Fifthly, *the teaching of Scripture.* When we look to the Bible for guidance on this subject we find that the biblical writers are conscious of God's hand upon them long before birth. Think of the birth stories that go back long before conception: how many individuals – such as Samuel, Samson, Jacob and Esau and Jeremiah – were either called by God, or were spoken of in advance, long before the moment of their natural birth. This does not make the case unanswerable, but it is an important factor …

But what *does*, in my opinion, conclusively resolve the issue is the use of the Greek word *brephos* in Luke 1.41. It means "the child". "The child leaped in her womb" – it is the same word as is used for a child *after* birth. And, more than leaping in her womb, the child apparently was filled with the Holy Spirit. Elizabeth spoke of the pregnant Mary as the "mother of my Lord".

This brings us therefore to the Christian affirmation of the incarnation, which leaves us no room for escape at all. If you are an orthodox, well-taught Christian who is asked, "When did God become man?" you will respond with the Apostles' Creed: "conceived by the Holy Ghost, born of the Virgin Mary". That is when he became man [at conception].

But if that is true, then manhood [or human existence] begins at conception. And if the proper man – that is, Jesus – began his earthly existence as a human being at conception, then so do all human beings. It is inescapable.

Raymond's desperate concern over abortion was ultimately from his understanding that God has created men and women in his own image.

But Raymond's Reformed instincts also meant that he was not only concerned with the individual. He was also concerned with those social groups that God had ordained either at creation or as part of his providential ordering of the world – in particular the State and the Family with married parents.

And Raymond's Reformed instincts meant that he was concerned for the preaching and teaching of the law as well as the gospel. He knew that without the law there was no gospel. If people did not know they were guilty before God, why would they want a Saviour - except as an add-on to make life more comfortable? He believed that the Reformers had got it right when they spoke about the law's "threefold function":

> Firstly, it restrained sin and preserved order; secondly, it brought home to a man that he was personally responsible for his conduct, and above all, to God, and thus created conviction of sin, and, thirdly, it guided the Christian in his conduct.

And the law was supremely summed up in the Ten Commandments:

> The Decalogue (the ten commandments) represents the permanent and universal decrees of the Sovereign Creator for mankind

And Raymond knew that God had written the law in two places, not only on tablets of stone, but also as Paul says in Romans in the human heart. And God's moral law is not an "alien intrusion but there is a fundamental correspondence between God's moral law and our human being" (to quote John Stott). In simpler terms, God's law is "the maker's instructions". So when we obey it, we are working with the grain of the created order. Because that is so, there is a general awareness of a basic moral law or "natural law". Therefore, in moral campaigns you can have alliances with people who may not as yet be believers, but who are aware of God's moral law, given by God's common grace (not his saving grace) and given through general revelation (not special revelation – in the Bible).

So Raymond Johnston was rooted in the Bible and the 16th Century Reformers.

Focused on cultural disintegration

Focused on cultural disintegration

In his thinking on the wider issues of the state and society, Raymond was absolutely convinced that what you believe does have social consequences.

A moral vision is needed to inspire a people to give them coherence and identity and purpose … Some – in particular, many of the Eastern religions – cherish the distant possibility of merging with the Infinite. In the West, we have looked for centuries at the picture of a man dying on a cross, giving himself for his fellow men … These visions which shape moral beliefs are very different in different societies. But because they determine what we think about the purpose of life, they have tremendous inspirational power.

And of relevance for this time particularly, Autumn 2001, Raymond has some observations on Islam. In his book *Who Needs the Family* he is writing about Fatherhood. He then says this:

There is … a religious "skew" latent in Judaism itself and fully developed in Islam. This is the blazing, oppressive, dynamic, ultra-masculine character of Allah – the one true God to the Muslim. Springing from a Near Eastern and Jewish environment, but rejecting the deity of Christ and the Trinitarian nature of God, the Prophet proclaimed a God characterized by a crushing sense of "otherness". In contemplating this God we are overwhelmed by a consciousness of undifferentiated *power* which swallows up the truly personal, relational aspect known to Christians when they speak of God as Father. The spread of this Unitarian ethical monotheism is an impressive cultural achievement. But the ninety-nine attributes and names of Allah do not include love, and the impenetrable unity of the nature of the divine Being demands only submission – a fatalistic acceptance of all events, as man bows before the incomprehensible. This dominant theocratic creed can be seen as hyper-masculinity projected into the image of God – a new idolatry once more. And it is not surprising therefore to find that in countries where Islam's teaching has deeply influenced the laws and conventions, the status of woman is very low. Professor Anderson indeed has spoken of the "degradation of Muslim womanhood." Nor are we surprised to discover in Islam's teaching the doctrine of the Jihad or holy war – another manifestation of religiously sanctioned ultra-aggressiveness …

Raymond Johnston was fully aware that the Christian needed not just to be concerned with "politics" when he or she focused on the wider world. He knew that the Public Square was bigger than Parliament Square. He saw the vital need to come to terms with the whole issue of "culture". But what is culture? He offered this as a definition:

> [Culture is] a persisting pattern of thinking, feeling, believing and evaluating, socially acquired by learning as distinct from biologically inherited, through which the cumulative heritage and value systems of a society are transmitted, and by virtue of which both individual meanings and social institutions cohere and continue.

Obviously, then, a culture can be according to God's Word, against God's word, neutral or mixed. And obviously cultures can be in various states of moral health. Raymond's contention was that we in the West are now living in a "collapsing culture". He argued that there "has been the decline of shared moral and spiritual convictions". So he asked the question: "What is our Christian duty in this situation?"

Now Raymond was very aware of the dangers of the so-called "social gospel":

At the very deepest level Christian testimony in any age is always the same. Take 1 John 1. Christian testimony asserts the facts that God is Light and that no man can say he is not a sinner; that the eternal Word of Life was with the Father from all eternity yet has become incarnate; that through the blood of Jesus Christ men and women can now be cleansed from sin, since God is faithful and just to forgive us our sins, and that when he forgives us we begin to enjoy fellowship with him, with his Son and with each other, and we experience great joy. These things are part of the unalterable Good News and we find them all in that one seminal chapter.

But he went on to make the following points:

> Yet if this is *all* we "see" in Holy Scripture and in church history, we fall somewhat short of the whole counsel of God.

The Bible has a lot to teach about social and cultural life. And faithfulness to the Bible in these matters does change societies and cultures:

> It is not simply that there are converts and heaven rejoices with the church as she grows [he wrote]. When the gospel prospers something else is given to a nation besides individual believers. The whole quality of social life is changed as more and more people apply the Word of God to their own life in the community. In this respect many of us are glad to point out to our doubting friends that seventeenth century England was in many ways a better society after the Reformers and the Puritans, eighteenth century England a healthier place thanks to Whitfield and Wesley, nineteenth century England ennobled by the work of Spurgeon and the others.

But his desperate concern was over what he saw as cultural collapse. And the culture he saw collapsing was our own Western culture with its threefold roots in …

> … [first] the questioning of the Greeks; [secondly] the organization and sense of law of the Romans, and thirdly (and most important) the Judaeo-Christian religious and moral contribution. This last influence has been the

deepest formative principle in the development of Western European culture. It was this that brought us the dignity of woman, the sacredness of the family, the intellectual base for the rise of modern science, our hospitals, our schools, our universities and – if we are to believe even some of the non-Christian economists – our great economic take-off after the Reformation.

And what is a primary course of this collapse? Raymond was clear in his own mind:

> The most radical fault dates back a century – it is the lack of the fire and the vision of the gospel. Christianity in Britain has experienced a disastrous decline in the preaching and teaching of the Word of God. The church is weak, and the prevalent religious liberalism prevents her from preaching and expounding God's law. Without the law there is no understanding of the urgency and the glory of the New Testament gospel ..

Nor is this claim that our culture is collapsing just some subjective judgment on the part of super-sensitive people:

> This disintegration [says Raymond Johnston] can be evaluated by the Christian in a number of ways. Take Leviticus 18, which is part of the Mosaic legislation. It is a frightening study to go through that chapter and ask "How is this word of God judging our culture today?" Those things prohibited to the Israelites as abominations, things which were not even to be named or considered amongst them are all back with us ... The chapter goes on to mention homosexuality, behaviour which is now openly propagated in magazines, and approved or at least tolerated by an increasing group of men in a number of churches ... Leviticus goes on to forbid sexual intercourse between humans and animals – things which can now be seen on the cinema screen in New York and Denmark and can be found in magazines available in this country. These are the enormities that are with us, every one of them forbidden in that one chapter ... They pollute the whole community and the very region where they are prevalent – "the land is defiled" (v 25)

… Any man of God with his Bible open will view with the utmost seriousness the eighteenth and nineteenth chapters of Genesis, which record the destruction of Sodom. He will also note that the first chapter of the Epistle to the Romans condemns the sin of sodomy in a particular terrifying way. We are not speaking here of tendencies or temptations … What Scripture condemns is the deliberate satisfaction of homosexual desire in forbidden behaviour – sodomy … Homosexual indulgence is something which God condemns as the ultimate sign of decadence and degradation in any culture.

So how are we to respond?

A call for Christian thinking and action

Raymond Johnston went back to the sack of Rome as having something to teach us today:

> I have always been very moved by these words which I read in a church history book: "on the 24th August in the Year of the City 1164, and in the year of our Lord Jesus Christ 410, the Goths under Alaric entered and sacked Rome. 'My voice sticks in my throat,' says Jerome, 'and sobs choke me as I dictate. The city which took the whole world captive is itself taken.' Jerome uttered the sensations of all, both Christian and heathen. There has been no such shock to Europe since." So wrote Charles Williams in *The Descent of the Dove*. (We do well to remember that the last sentence was written in 1939 before we opened the doors of Belsen, Dachau and Buchenwald). The sack of Rome sent a tremor throughout Christianity; Jerome's words show a Christian feeling deeply the collapse of a culture.

So the first response of a Christian is to show compassion at such a time

> As a culture collapses people get hurt. If my love for my neighbour means anything to me at all, the fact that my neighbour and my neighbour's children are now open to subtle forms of media-controlled, psychologically-dominated poison must surely make me feel sorrow and compassion for them.

Nor was Raymond Johnston concerned just to quote texts and be prophetic. He was also concerned to argue and use anthropology and sociology to confirm God's truth.

Take for example the issues of sex and marriage. Raymond was concerned to make public the findings of what had happened in the 1920s in Soviet Russia when the Leninists attempted to abolish family ties completely and when:

> … marriage became civil registration only, and that in a most undignified and hole-in-corner way. Divorce became possible by simple declaration. Incest, bigamy and adultery ceased to be criminal offences. Abortion on request was made possible without the necessity even to declare a reason, and a little later the labour laws made it obligatory for people to accept any post imposed on them, wherever that job might be. No modification was conceded even in the case of a husband posted away from his wife, or a wife sent to employment away from her husband. As a result of these policies family ties were weaker by 1930. But other effects were also noticed. By 1935 it was clear that the nation had been enfeebled and that it could not call upon such strong and widespread popular allegiance in the case of a possible war. The specific results of the anti-family policy were serious. Free divorce and abortion had pushed down the birth rate. In 1934 in the hospitals of Moscow there were 53,000 births and 154,000 abortions. Juvenile delinquency, violence in schools, vandalism, sadistic behaviour by quite young children – all these things had spread … [So] from 1935 onwards the process was put in reverse … Marriage became desirable and children were taught from their earliest years that it was a serious matter, a commitment for life. One article records an interesting sign: in 1936 wedding rings re-appeared in the shops of Moscow

He also wanted to make public the findings of the anthropologist, J.D.Unwin. Unwin wrote a massive book in 1934 entitled *Sex and Culture*:

> Unwin describes his investigation as follows:
> When I started these researches I sought to establish nothing, and had no idea of what the result would be. With care-free open-mindedness I decided

to test, by a reference to human records, a somewhat startling conjecture that had been made by the analytical psychologists. This suggestion was that if the social regulations forbid direct satisfaction of the sexual impulses the emotional conflict is expressed in another way, and that what we call "civilization" has always been built up by compulsory sacrifices in the gratification of innate desires.

Unwin selected only societies for which sufficient evidence could be found (a) of sexual regulation and (b) of what he calls "cultural energy". This latter he defined as a process perceived as tending towards questioning, exploring and conquering. His studies covered eighty primitive societies and sixteen civilized societies and his two general conclusions were as follows:

1.   The cultural condition of any society in any geographical environment is conditioned by its past and present methods of regulating the relations between the sexes.

2.   No society can display productive social energy unless a new generation inherits a social system under which sexual opportunity is reduced to a minimum.

The Western Christian norm received [says Raymond Johnston] startling support from this research. *The greatest energy*, Unwin comments, *has been displayed only by those societies which have reduced their sexual opportunity to a minimum by the adoption of absolute monogamy.*

… [Unwin] concluded that the evidence pointed towards a choice: either cultural energy and achievement, or sexual licence. It is impossible for any society to enjoy *both* for more than one generation. Aldous Huxley examined Unwin's evidence in his book *Ends and Means* (1965), as did Dr David Mace, and both found his evidence compelling. The way in which Unwin's work has been almost completely ignored by both scholars and popular writers sometimes seems positively sinister.

So concludes Raymond Johnston.

Now, in responding to the problems relating to cultural and social life he knew that he had to fight not only opponents in the world, but also opponents in the church who were wrongly "pietistic".

But Raymond Johnston was adamant. Jesus prayed not that his disciples would be taken out of the world but that they would be protected from the evil one (John 17.15). So we must avoid what he called "Christian insulation":

The desire to be a hermit or to enter the monastery [he said] is not one which belongs solely to the Roman tradition.

Indeed, Raymond's biblical heroes were Joseph and Daniel – men who remained faithful while at the heart of public life.

We need, therefore, to revive the concept of "Christian citizenship" which, he claimed, "has almost died over the last hundred years."

It was there in Victorian England, particularly towards the beginning of the century. Yet in the second half of the nineteenth century it gradually died. It must be revived. Here is an urgent teaching ministry for today, if ever there was one. We can approach this on the lowest level possible first, that of sheer opportunity. We live in a democracy, which means that every man's and woman's voice counts. We have a vote locally and a vote nationally. We can write letters which have a chance of being printed, we can make ourselves heard in all sorts of ways … Are we not under a clear obligation to participate and to use our voice for the standards which we know God has revealed?

His argument was simple. If "God is concerned with guiding nations", so must we be. If God has made us stewards of the created order, we must exercise that stewardship. If God has revealed to his people the truth about social righteousness, they must pass that revelation on. If they are to be salt and light in the world, so be it. And he wrote this:

We are commanded by the Apostle Paul to pray for good government (1 Timothy 1.2-4). How could we conceive that God would ask all his people to pray for something, and then respond by saying that of course the answer can only come through the ungodly!

No! Christian people are to think and then be active. First, they are to "use the Word of God to identify evil". Secondly, they are "to try to understand the times and channels by which evil is spread":

So we ask ourselves "How is Satan active? How is he getting this grip on our culture, splintering, fragmenting and poisoning it?" ... The press, books and magazines, film and theatre, radio and TV – the media – are paramount. Then at a deeper level we need to study the attacks upon institutions – the family, school and the legal system ... All these have been deeply penetrated by Satanic forces in the last two or three decades.

Thirdly, they are "never [to] reject alliances":

Where there are other Christians – even where there are non-Christians – who on a specific issue will denounce a manifest evil and determine to fight it, there we have a platform on which others may make common cause with us. As unashamed Christians we make no apology for our reasons in what we are doing. We tell the others, any audience we address or any group we organize, that we are in this fight because we are the servants of the Lord Jesus Christ. We confess that the law of God, our loving Father, forbids these things; we know that they will only bring cruelty, suffering and chaos. We make no bones about our allegiance, for we are men under authority. Yet at the same time we can say to others, "If you will join with us to fight this we welcome you."

Fourthly, as we have seen, they are to "get to grips with the intellectual debate." Fifthly, they are to realize that there is a spiritual battle going on. So there must be prayer. And, sixthly, they are "to strengthen the things that remain":

It is possible that our culture may collapse as did the culture of Rome. We know that the church of Jesus Christ will still persist, because we have his promise that the gates of hell cannot prevail against it (Matt 16.18) ... But meanwhile it is our responsibility to arrest [the] decay wherever we can, to fight the pollution that is at present being publicly disseminated into the families of our land, and particularly to our children ... Not everyone can do everything and some people can do nothing but pray (which may well turn out to be the most important ministry of all!). But many, many more could be doing far more than they are doing.

The root cause of the moral decline and cultural disintegration of Britain is undoubtedly to be found in the failure of the professing churches to testify to the goodness and severity of God, to the awesome Creator whose holiness convicts us but whose grace provides a wonderful pardon and restoration at the cost of the blood of the Divine Son. Failure to preach and to live by this gospel deprives a society of the preservative "salt" which the church is commanded to become.

Yet there is a mute rebuke to many of those who have remained faithful to the apostolic faith of the New Testament. It lies in our Lord's best known parable. The orthodox were so concerned with their religious tasks that they passed by on the other side, while the heretic was the man who saw the wounded traveller and had compassion, went to him and bound up his wounds, pouring in oil and wine, and set him on his beast and brought him to an inn and took care of him.

Two things angered Raymond Johnston, first, the false teaching of heretics and, secondly, the passivity of the faithful.

So following Raymond Johnston, in God's strength, let us seek to be faithful and then to be active and not passive.